30 Days with a Great S...

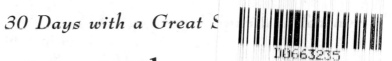

Love Without Measure

■ ■ ■ ■ ■ ■ ■ ■ ■ ■ ■ ■

The Spirituality of Service of

MOTHER TERESA

JOHN KIRVAN

ave maria press AmP Notre Dame, Indiana

JOHN KIRVAN, who conceived this series and has authored most of its titles, writes primarily about classical spirituality. Other recent books include *God Hunger, Silent Hope, Raw Faith,* and *There Is a God, There Is No God.*

www.avemariapress.com

International Standard Book Number: 1-59471-025-2

Cover and text design by Katherine Robinson Coleman

Printed and bound in the United States of America.

Library of Congress Cataloging-in-Publication Data
Kirvan, John J.
  Love without measure : the spirituality of service of Mother Teresa / John Kirvan.
    p. cm. — (Thirty days with a great spiritual teacher)
  ISBN 1-59471-025-2 (pbk.)
 1. Teresa, Mother, 1910—Meditations. 2. Catholic Church—Prayer-books and devotions—English. I. Title. II. Series: 30 days with a great spiritual teacher.

  BX4406.5.Z8K57 2004
  242'.2—dc22

                    2004006264

Contents

Love cannot remain by itself,
it has no meaning.
Love has to be put into action
and that action is service.

MOTHER TERESA

Whatever you do for the least of these,
my brothers and sisters,
you do for me.

JESUS OF NAZARETH

Mother Teresa of Calcutta
(1910–1997)

On September 10, 1946, Mother Teresa, born Agnes Gonxha Bojaxhiu in Skopje, Macedonia, was thirty-seven years old. She had been a nun in final vows for just over ten years, a teacher of children for over twenty years, and by her own description, the happiest member of her religious order, the Sisters of Loretto.

But that day, traveling by train between Calcutta and Darjeeling, she began a journey that would take her into another world—the world of the destitute and the dying. And celebrity.

She became intensely aware that men, women, and children were dying untended on the streets of India. She felt a call not only to care for them, but to leave the shelter of her convent life to live among them.

No one, she believed, should die without ever knowing that they are loved. Her mission became to take that conviction, that love to the streets of Calcutta. At first she was alone in her mission. It would take several years before another woman shared her vision deeply enough to join with her in the beginning of what was to become a new religious order dedicated to turning love of the destitute into a life of service— vowed not only to poverty, chastity, and obedience, but to "wholehearted, free service to the poorest of the poor."

In an amazingly short time her plain white, blue-trimmed sari, now worn by thousands, became a sign of hope and practical service in dozens of countries and multitudes of lives.

From one point of view her story from this time on becomes a simple but astonishing tale of institutional growth fired by faith. And except for its magnitude not an unusual story.

But something else was happening.

Mother Teresa had become a household name—for its own reasons the world embraced her.

The government of India honored her with the Order of the Lotus and granted her life-long Indian citizenship. Southeast

Asia Treaty Organization gave her the Magsaysay award. Paul VI invited her to open a center in Rome. She received the Good Samaritan award, the Templeton Award for progress in religion, the Pope John XXIII Peace Prize, and the most prestigious recognition, the Nobel Peace Prize. In time President Clinton made her an honorary U.S. citizen because she had "brought hope and love into the lives of millions of orphaned and abandoned children the world over." She was welcomed in Cuba, in Moscow, in countries that abhor religion.

Something was going on.

Prince Philip would say it as well as anyone.

"I do not believe," he said in awarding her the Templeton Prize, "there is any other way of measuring faith except through daily actions and behavior. No ceremonies, no protestations, no displays, no routines of prayer, and no theorizing can compare with the smallest act of genuine and practical compassion as a true reflection of personal faith."

In the end it is compassion embodied in service that makes a life worth living. Saints—everyday believers—are measured not by their sermonizing but by how they treat the poor.

The world embraced Teresa of Calcutta because they recognized in her someone who lived truthfully the values that we only professed.

We looked at her and said: "That's the way it should be."

We honored her and felt better for it. And then, as often as not, we went on our way.

But in the light of her life we could never again say, "I believe," without hearing the voice of the poor.

The voice of Agnes Gonxha Bojaxhiu.

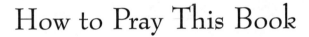

How to Pray This Book

The purpose of this book is to open a gate for its readers, to make accessible the spiritual experience and wisdom of one of the modern world's best known spiritual teachers—and practitioners, Mother Teresa of Calcutta. Specifically it is designed to spell out her special message—the inseparable roles that faith and service must play in any healthy spirituality. It is a theme often neglected in the history of spirituality with its traditional emphasis on the contemplative, monastic tradition and what must seem at times a resultant short-changing of the role of service in any healthy spiritual life.

This modern Teresan spirituality is an ongoing dialogue of street service and scripture, an ongoing dialogue of faith and works, an unapologetic dialogue of a nun and belief in Jesus.

The thing is, unlike so many mystics and saints, Mother Teresa said and wrote very little. She did much.

This book is an opportunity to reflect upon and pray about a life, a spirituality of service. It is about what it is like to live a life where service and love are interchangeable terms.

Teresan spirituality is a tale of scripture coming alive in the street.

My day begins with faith,

and comes alive through service.

This, therefore, is not a book for mere reading. It invites you to meditate and pray its words on a daily basis over a period of thirty days. More to the point, it invites you to put those acts of faith into action, putting your faith at the service of those most in need. To bring to life the basic truth that whatever we do for these, the least of our brothers and sisters, we do for Jesus. Whatever we fail to do, we fail to do for Jesus.

It is a handbook for a spiritual journey in a world that is desperately in need.

Before you read the "rules" for taking this spiritual journey, remember that this book is meant to free your spirit, not to confine it. If on any day the meditation does not resonate well for you, turn elsewhere to find a passage that seems to best fit the spirit of your day and your soul. Don't hesitate to repeat a day as often as you like until you feel that you have discovered what the Spirit, through the words of the author, has to say to your spirit.

Here are suggestions on one way to use this book as a cornerstone of your prayers.

As Your Day Begins

As the day begins set aside a quiet moment in a quiet place to read the meditation suggested for the day.

The passage is short. It never runs more than a couple of hundred words, but it has been carefully selected to give a spiritual focus, a spiritual center to your whole day. It is designed to remind you as another day begins of your own existence at a spiritual level. It is meant to put you in the presence of the spiritual master who is your companion and teacher on this journey. But most of all the purpose of the passage is to remind you that at this moment and at every moment during this day you will be living and acting in the presence of a God who invites you continually but quietly to live in and through him.

A word of advice: read slowly. Very slowly. The meditation has been broken down into sense lines to help you do just this. Don't read to get to the end, but to savor each part of the meditation. You never know what short phrase, what word will trigger a response in your spirit. Give the words a chance. After all you are not just reading this passage, you are praying it. You are establishing a mood of serenity for your whole day. What's the rush?

All Through Your Day

Immediately following the day's reading you will find a single sentence which we have chosen to call a mantra, a word borrowed from the Hindu tradition. This phrase is meant as a companion for your spirit as it moves through a busy day. Write it down on a 3" x 5" card or on the appropriate page of your daybook. Look at it as often as you can. Repeat it quietly to yourself—and go on your way.

It is not meant to stop you in your tracks or to distract you from responsibilities but simply, gently, to remind you of the presence of God and your desire to respond to this presence.

As Your Day Is Ending

This is a time for letting go of the day.

Find a quiet place and quiet your spirit. Breathe deeply.

Inhale, exhale—slowly and deliberately, again and again until you feel your body let go of its tension.

Now read the evening prayer slowly, phrase by phrase. You may recognize at once that we have taken one of the most familiar evening prayers of the Christian tradition and woven into it phrases taken from the meditation with which you began your day and the mantra that has accompanied you all through your day. In this way, a simple evening prayer gathers together the spiritual character of the day that is now ending as it began—in the presence of God.

It is a time for summary and closure.

Invite God to embrace you with love and to protect you through the night.

Sleep well.

Some Other Ways to Use This Book

1. Use it any way your spirit suggests. As mentioned earlier, skip a passage that doesn't resonate for you on a given day, or repeat for a second day or even several days a passage whose richness speaks to you. The truths of a spiritual life are not absorbed in a day, or for that matter, in a lifetime. So take your time. Be patient with the Lord. Be patient with yourself.

2. Take two passages and/or their mantras—the more contrasting the better—and "bang" them together. Spend time discovering how their similarities or differences illumine your path.

3. Start a spiritual journal to record and deepen your experience of this thirty-day journey. Using either the mantra or another phrase from the reading that appeals to you, write a spiritual

account of your day, a spiritual reflection. Create your own meditation.

4. Join millions who are seeking to deepen their spiritual life by joining with others to form a small group. More and more people are doing just this to support each other in their mutual quest. Meet once a week, or at least every other week to discuss and pray about one of the meditations. There are many books and guides available to help you make such a group effective.

Thirty Days With
Mother Teresa

Where is the face of God to whom I can pray?
The answer is simple.
That naked one,
that lonely one,
that unwanted one,
is my brother and my sister.

MOTHER TERESA

Day One

My Day Begins

"The world today is hungry,
not only for bread
but hungry for love,
hungry to be wanted,
to be loved."

■

There is nothing new about poverty
and the hunger that comes with it.
There is nothing new about hunger
and the invisibility that comes with it.

There is nothing new about the invisibility
of those who have nothing
and the blindness of those who have something,
who have everything.
There is nothing new about the prayer of the poor.
Look at me.
There are millions of us.
But each of us has a name.
See me.
Know that I exist.
Know that what you feel, I feel.
Know that I hunger for bread,
but not just for bread.
Know that I am hungry to be wanted,
hungry to be loved.
Know that I am.

But this is a tricky turn in the road.
It is easy for us to convince ourselves
that love is a substitute for bread,
or that bread is a substitute for love,
that feeling "bad,"
overwhelmed, and confused
is a substitute
for both love and bread.

It is easy for us to convince ourselves
that not knowing which way to turn
is an excuse for not turning at all,
an excuse for standing still
and hoping the poor will go away,
their prayers heard by someone
with more to give.

All Through the Day

I am. See me. Hear me.

My Day Is Ending

Here in the growing darkness of this night
you are waiting to be fed.

Here in the growing silence of this night
you are waiting to know that you are loved.

I know that you are here.

You are the poor
and you are always with us,
always hungry,
and not only for bread.
But I am tired at this day's end.
It has left me empty,
hungry for rest.

My eyes want to close.

I want to tell you
to come back in the morning
when I have the energy of a new day.

But you are here now.
And your hunger won't wait.
Can't wait.

You are waiting to be fed.
Hungry for bread,
but not for bread alone.

Bring in the poor and the hungry.
Don't bother.
They're here.

Day Two

My Day Begins

"Poverty doesn't only consist
of being hungry for bread,
but rather it is a tremendous hunger
for human dignity."

Mother Teresa knew
what the people of Calcutta were missing.
Food—of course.
A roof over their head—certainly.
Someone to hold them

when disease ate away their bodies
and their dignity,
when death seemed their only certainty.
Their only release.

But she also knew of their hunger
for something,
for someone
who would reach out to them
through the emptiness
and anonymity of the streets
and call them
by their name.

Someone who would love them unconditionally.

She knew of their hunger for God
and what only God could give.

And she knew of God's hunger for them.
Beneath their shattered dignity
was someone loved unconditionally by God.
In a dying beggar,
Hungry, homeless, in pain,
she saw God.

But she never lost sight
of human beings
hungry for bread,
living without shelter
on the city's cruel streets.

All Through the Day

God is where you find him.

My Day Is Ending

Here in the deepening silence of this night
it is easy for me
to slip into a feel-good world,
where some soft-centered prayers for the poor
will be enough
to take away their hunger
and settle my debt,
to sleep untroubled
by the streets,
my dignity intact
will come too easily.

Your children are hungry,
Naked and homeless.

So many of them will die tonight.
So many of them
alone and nameless.
I will be helpless,
but hopefully not oblivious.
I know that my feel good prayers
will not be enough.

But there is tomorrow.
There is hope for them,
and for me.

Day Three

My Day Begins

"Love has to be put in action
and that action is service."

■

What is there about us
that expects
our spiritual journey
will begin and end in a bath of warm feelings?

In our heart we know that it won't be like this.

It is about a special kind of love
that Mother Teresa has defined for us.
It is a love that serves.

We watch this tiny, seemingly frail woman
walk a Calcutta street.
She sees a homeless mother and child.
She finds shelter for them.
For men and women
huddled on a street corner
without hope,
waiting to die,
she finds a bed
and someone who cares.
Someone to hold their hand.

She teaches us what it is to love,
not in words,
but in actions of stark and life challenging simplicity.

It can't, we think, be this simple.
But it is.

Love is a synonym for service.
When we serve our brothers and sisters
we put our lives at the service of God.

And through our hands,
those in need
are touched by love,
are touched by God.

All Through the Day

Love serves.

My Day Is Ending

Here in the deepening silence of this night
remind me again
that to love is to serve,
that to serve is to love.

Remind me
that I cannot reach out to you
unless I reach out to the least of these,
my brothers and sisters.

Remind me
that when I reach out to them,
I am reaching out to you.

So let their voices—
let your voice—

break through
my deafness to their pain.

Remind me
that a simple gesture of human caring
is a miracle.
It is enough to reach your ears,
enough to temper their pain.

Day Four

My Day Begins

"Knowledge can only lead to love
and love to service."

■

Mother Teresa is one of the last people in the world
that you would expect to find making excuses
for the indifference of the rich.

"The trouble is," she said,
"that rich people, well-to-do people,
very often don't really know who the poor are."

Not knowing the poor by name,
not knowing the world in which they live,
they remained untouched—
we remain untouched—
by the reality of their lives,
by the reality of poverty,
of hunger,
of lack of shelter,
by the painful struggle
just to stay alive.

And where there is no knowledge,
there is no love.
Where there is no love,
there is no helping hand.

We keep our distance
from those who are most in need.
We remain untouched
by those we do not know,
our heart protected from their need.

We live in a sheltered world.
And because we do not know the poor,
we do not love them.
And because we do not love them
we do not feel their pain.

Our knowledge never becomes love.
Our love never becomes service.

All Through the Day

We do not love what we do not know.

My Day Is Ending

Here in the deepening silence of this night
I admit that I am seeking shelter
from the voices of the poor,
from the pain of the streets

I am afraid to go there.

If I seek out the poor as she did,
I will have to come to know them
as she knew them,
to love them as she loved them,
to serve them as she served them,
and I am not ready.

Not yet.
Perhaps not ever.

But for now
come to me
in the silence of this night
and bring to me
the courage I need
here in the darkness,
the courage of Mother Teresa,
her love,
her willingness to serve.

In the night
that is just now beginning,
let me catch a glimpse
of that frail, strong woman,
and for just a moment
face the coming day
unafraid of her poor.

Day Five

My Day Begins

"We have to be aware of the poor in order to love them."

It is not a matter of
not feeling the pain
of the poor.
It is a matter of not even seeing them,
not seeing the hunger that is there,
that cries out for our attention.

Most of us
can justifiably plead
ignorance, blindness, deafness.
We don't see.
Not because we can't see,
but because we don't look.

Our eyes, our hearts, are somewhere else.

"It is very easy,"
an American first lady remarked
after a meeting with Mother Teresa,
"for us who inhabit this rich, affluent global economy
to turn a blind eye to the needs
of the poorest of the poor.

But because she was willing and able
to show us where they lived,
where they suffered,
where they are needed,
we can never walk away again."
"Look," Mother Teresa said.
"If you wish to see God . . . look at his poor."

It is such an ancient truth,
one that is at the heart of Jesus' teaching.
But there is no question
that in every generation, in every life,
especially in our own,
we need to hear it repeated loudly and clearly:
God is there for those who look.

All Through the Day

There are no excuses for walking away.

My Day Is Ending

I walk through the days of my life,
with my eyes wide open
and I see nothing
but what I expect to see.
I walk by you
without seeing you.
I know that it is
a matter of looking.

I walk now
into the darkness of this night
hoping to see you.

But first I must open my eyes
to what is there, to who is there.

Then I must look to where you point,
to where you are,
to where Mother Teresa looked,
to see what she saw . . .
a man dying in the street,
a millionaire,
a sinner,
a saint.
Each of them is precious to God.

And then
in the darkness of this night
your face may appear.

Day Six

My Day Begins

"We are precious to him.
that man dying in the street—precious to him,
that millionaire—precious to him,
that sinner—precious to him."

God loves us all.
And we are without exception meant to love one another.
Mother Teresa knew and lived this.
It was the driving force at the center of her life and works,
the heart of the message she conveyed to her sisters

and to the millions of people whose spiritual imagination
was and still is caught up
by her life of service to those in need.
God loves us all.
And we are to love one another.
A blazingly simple truth that is easy to forget.
That man dying out of sight on a city street
is precious to him. To us.
The oblivious young man who walks on by
is precious to him. To us.
So too the young woman who stops to call for help
is precious to him. To us.
But no more than the sinner.

We are all precious to him.
He loves us all.
No one more than another.

But in our times some more than others
need a helping hand.
We need to be reminded of the needs
of a world beyond our immediate vision,
of an overlooked world of pain and suffering
as close as our neighbor, as close as our own family,
as distant as the evening news.

We easily forget. We easily ignore.

But in the early morning hours of any given day,
of this day,
Mother Teresa is there to remind us.
It is then that we need to hear again
and accept her simple words:
We are precious to God—and to each other.

◆◆◆◆◆

All Through the Day

We are, all of us, precious to him.

◆◆◆◆◆

My Day Is Ending

Here as the night begins
And I seek the silence and peace of sleep,
I do not need to remind you
who I am,
what I have done,
what I have left undone,
how rich or poor I am.

None of this matters.
I just am.
And this is enough
for you.
But this also is true:
As this night begins,

I am not hungry,
but others are.
I am free,
but others are not.

We share this:
We are loved by God.
We are precious to him.

But love cannot remain by itself.
By itself it has no meaning.
Love has to be put in action
And that action is service.

Day Seven

My Day Begins

"Where Jesus is there is joy.
Where Jesus is there is love.
Where Jesus is there is peace."

A Calcutta street seems hardly the place
to look for peace, for joy, for love.
In some sheltered convent somewhere perhaps,
but on a Calcutta street, hardly.
Or on my street.
But Mother Teresa
knew it was there

waiting to be discovered,
waiting to be unchained.

She knew it was there,
because Jesus,
the core of her life,
was there,
had always been there,
was still there
waiting to be released in lives
that seemed
so distant from peace and joy and love,
strangers to hope.

Mother Teresa did not bring hope to the dying.
She announced its presence,
celebrated its reality,
released its power,
became its servant.

LOVE WITHOUT MEASURE

We are not talking about joy
that is just some kind of bubbly good feeling,
about peace that is no more than trouble-free days,
about love that never gets beyond splashes of warmth.

We are talking about a layer of hope
that takes root in our souls,
that is there even on days
when there is not that much to be happy about,
even on streets that are strangers to hope.

That woman in white
on the streets of Calcutta
redefined hope for another generation
by reminding us of a presence
that is too easy to forget
when hope becomes a stranger.

All Through the Day

Hope need not be a stranger.

LOVE WITHOUT MEASURE

My Day Is Ending

Here in the growing darkness
I can feel hope slipping away into the night.

This long day,
this long year has
all but eaten away my fragile hope.
One headline at a time,
it has left me wordless in the dark.

As this night begins
I look for some way
to silence its dark message.

Tell me:
How did you hold on to hope
on the hopeless streets of Calcutta?

What did you know
that I must come to know
if my hope is to survive the night?

How did you know that there was joy
in the pain-ridden streets,
that there was peace and love,
where others found only despair?

How did you know where to look for hope?

How did you know it was already there?

Day Eight

My Day Begins

"Jesus has said to us very clearly:
I am the love with which you love."

■

There are two ways in which Mother Teresa saw Jesus at work
in everything she did.
She saw Jesus present
in everyone to whom she reached out.
But on the other hand she knew
that in everything she did,

it was Jesus reaching out through her.

"It is not I," she could say.
"It is Jesus at work in and through me."

"I am the love with which you love."

It was the clear spiritual vision of a woman
who may seem at first glance to be
more activist than mystic,
but who was in fact
a living affirmation
that mystics are not confined
within monastery walls.

She understood
that the love with which she loved,
the love that permeated every act of service,

was not of her making.
It was the love of Jesus at work
in and through her.

His is the love with which she loved
with which we love.

Our love, our service,
will not be of our making.
It will be the unearned
gift of God.

◆◆◆◆

All Through the Day

He is the love with which we love.

◆◆◆◆

My Day Is Ending

Here in the deepening silence of this night,
put your words
on my lips.

You are the love to be loved.
You are the life to be lived.
You are the joy to be shared.
You are the bread to be eaten.
You are the blood to be drunk.
You are the truth to be told.
You are the light to be lit.
You are the peace to be given.

Remind me with every word
that this night belongs not to me

but to you.
You are everything.

Let me understand
that my words are your words,
that with whatever love I love
it is your love.

Whatever love marks any act of service
is not of my making.
It is and always will be
the love of Jesus at work
in and through me.

Day Nine

My Day Begins

"Every person is Christ for me
and since there is only one Jesus
that person is the one person
in the world at that moment."

Mother Teresa looked at the whole world
but saw it one person at a time,
and always the same person.
Whether it was that shelterless mother and child,
the millionaire, or the sinner made no difference.
She saw Jesus.

This is the key to the mystery
that she celebrated in the life of everyone she met.
The mystery that we must embrace
if we are to understand the spirituality of service
that she lived and taught.
It was not for her a matter of changing the millionaire
or the sinner
into someone or something else,
into someone or something more lovable.
She saw everyone as they were.
She loved everyone as they were.

She didn't say:
I'll think of you as Jesus and then you will be lovable.
She said: *You are already Jesus.*
And you are utterly loveable just as who you are.

This is what Mother Teresa meant when she said
that she lived in a person-to-person world:
Every person is Christ for me
and since there is only one Jesus
that person is the one person
in the world.
at that moment.

All Through the Day

Every person is Christ for me.

My Day Is Ending

Here in the deepening silence of this night
the darkness is full of voices
that want nothing more than to be heard.

I am here. I exist.
See me. Hear me.
I am one of them.
See me. Hear me.

But do not let me become
so caught up with my needs
that I blind and deafen myself
to the voices that surround me,
to all the voices that are yours.

Do not let me become so caught up in my own neediness
that I hear only my voice,
so caught up with "me"
that I let my voice drown out your voice
and all the voices that are your voice,
that beg to be heard
here in the darkness of this night.

Let me live rather as Mother Teresa lived,
in a world where
Every person is Christ for me
and since there is only one Jesus
that person is the one person
in the world.
at that moment.

Day Ten

My Day Begins

"What you say matters little.
How you live makes all the difference."

■

Let us admit it:
there is—if only from time to time—
a temptation to turn our spiritual journey
into a withdrawal from the human condition.
There can be a temptation
to leave behind the messy, demanding world

of the homeless and the hungry
to find God in a neater more comforting place.

There can be a temptation
to search for and serve God in the right words,
or in words alone,
a God separated from the
stuttering, stumbling humanity of the streets.
But in the end our journey is not about finding the right words,
or the right gestures.
It is not about a sanitized God
at the end of a sanitized journey.

It is about living humanly
when confronted with our humanity.

It is about opening our eyes to the world within us,
to all the selfishness and fear within and around us,
to all the hunger of our common humanity.

It is about embracing a humanity
from which we would gladly flee.

It is about embracing a homeless God
who insists on living on the street,
hungry and naked.

It is about seeing the street as Mother Teresa saw it,
coming to know:
What we say matters little.
How we live makes all the difference.

All Through the Day

How we live makes all the difference.

My Day Is Ending

Here in the deepening silence of this night
I want nothing more than
to leave this day behind.

But sleep does not come so easily.
I cannot chose to be deaf and blind.
I cannot forget,
I must not forget,
the streets where I walked today.

They will still be there
when I wake to a new day.
God will still be there.

And it will be the same homeless God
who will still insist on living on the street,
hungry and naked.

There is no way
to leave behind the messy, demanding world
of the homeless and the hungry
to find God
in a neater more comforting place.

God has chosen to be found and served
where we are least comfortable.

Day Eleven

My Day Begins

"God will use you to accomplish great things
on the condition that
you believe much more in his love
than in your own weakness."

The woman who traveled the world,
building institutions of compassion and hope as she went,
and a family of women to serve those in need
did so believing not in her strength,
but in her weakness.

She solicited wherever, from whomever,
the millions of dollars and millions of freely given hours
that her vision required,
but she knew that
it is not dollars but faith
that builds and sustains
a safety-net woven of service
for a world in pain.

It was not her work, but God's.

God could use her
to accomplish great things
because she
believed much more in his love
than in her weakness.

She believed
that in everything she dreamed

and accomplished
it was not her doing,
but the doing of God.

It was,
it always is,
even in the strongest of us,
God at work.

We are not talking about suitable gestures of humility.
of good spiritual manners,
we are talking about not fooling ourselves
about taking bows
for what we have not done,
for what we can never do.
We are talking about relying much more on his love
than on our weakness.

◆◆◆◆◆

All Through the Day

God's strength is my weakness.

◆◆◆◆◆

My Day Is Ending

Here in your presence
in the dark silence of the night,
I do not have to pretend
to be strong.
I do not have to tell myself
that you need me.

You do not need me,
but you can use me.

You can use me
to accomplish great things,
but only on the condition that
I rely much more on the strength of your love
than on my weakness,

that I make room
for your love
to do
what only your love can do.

But it is, I admit,
so much easier in the quiet solitude of the night
to admit my total dependence on you
than it is during the day
when the world measures us by our strengths.

For once
let me carry the truth of this night,
your strength, my weakness,
into the day to come.

Day Twelve

My Day Begins

"God is very much in love with us.
This is something
that our human mind cannot understand."

■

Nothing is more mysterious than love,
than loving,
than being loved.

We know how mysterious it is,
how unforeseeable,

how unpredictable,
how puzzling, how confusing,
how overwhelming
it can be.

So when Mother Teresa says
in utter simplicity
that God is very much in love with us,
we are caught off guard.

We are pulled into the mysterious core
of our relationship with God.
Caught up in a love
Beyond anything we have ever known.

God is very much in love with us!
Knowing ourselves as we do,
how can it be?

It is easier for us to believe
that God made the world than it is for us
to believe that this same God
loves us deeply, uniquely, unquestioningly.

But God does love in just that way.
That's what the mystery is all about.

God loves us, she reminds us, with a love that is
"unconditional,
tender,
forgiving,
and complete."
Knowing this
was Mother Teresa's secret.
Ours too—if we embrace it.

All Through the Day

God is very much in love with us.

My Day Is Ending

Here in the dark silence of this night
I listen with my whole being.
I strain in the silence to hear your voice.
But I am hard of hearing.

Mother Teresa says
you are very much in love with all of us.
She says that
you are very much in love with me.

How can this be?
It is hard for me believe.
Your love seems much too much
for such as me.

And it is.

But here in this silent darkness
I will take your word
that you love me dearly,
that I need not earn your love.

There is no way I ever could.

But I can accept your love
for what it is,
a gift beyond earning—
unconditional,
tender,
forgiving,
and complete.

Day Thirteen

My Day Begins

"Intense love does not measure.
It just gives."

■

Because we have been told in a hundred ways
that nothing is more important than love
we can spend a good part of our life
looking for a definition of this love
that is so important,
so central to our lives,
but so hard to find.

It's even hard to recognize.

Is this love, we wonder. *Is that*?

Mother Teresa points out the way of her love.

Intense love, she says,
or any degree of love for that matter,
does not measure,
or for that matter, define.
It just gives.

Love is giving without measuring.

There, we tell ourselves,
must be more to love than this.
But there isn't.

We spoil love
by cutting corners,
by holding back,
by measuring out our love in cautious bits.

It is only slowly,
that we come to understand and accept
that what Mother Teresa is telling us
is that love's other name is
"generosity."

Which is also
God's other name.

All Through the Day

God's other name is generosity.

My Day Is Ending

Here in the deepening silence of this night
it is easy for me
to love without measure.
Generosity comes easily in the dark.

But a few hours from now,
in the light of another day,
I'll begin to ration love.

I'll begin to act as though
there is not enough love to go around.

I know better.
But only in the dark.

By light of day

I am cautious, stingy,
afraid to spend my love.

Please, in that moment,
stop me in my tracks.

Remind me that for Mother Teresa
there was always enough love.

Remind me that I live through
the generosity of God,
that the gift he has given me
is meant to be given away.

Love is not for hoarding.

Day Fourteen

My Day Begins

"Jesus' love for us is
unconditional,
tender,
forgiving,
complete."

■

Jesus' love for us is unconditional.

Our own loves
are shaped and colored

by a raft of conditions.
Setting conditions to our loves
is in fact
one of the things
that we do best.

It's how we protect our hearts from disappointment.
It is how we protect ourselves against failure.
To be honest about it,
it is how we dodge
the unconditional love of God,
how we deafen ourselves
to the pain of others.
It is how we avoid the life
that Mother Teresa calls us to.
It is how we avoid those

on whose behalf she speaks,
all those she serves in love,
who wait on city streets
for our unconditioned love.
Who wait. And wait again.

Instead we come to them
weighted down with conditions.
We set conditions where there are none,
where there is only a call to unconditional love
and unconditional service.

All Through the Day

No conditions. None.

My Day Is Ending

Here in the dark silence of this night,
if only for a few quiet moments,
let me love you
as you love me,
as Mother Teresa loved you.

Let me love you
unconditionally.

Show me how to live without the conditions,
that color and flood my every prayer,
all the days and nights of my life.

Show me how to love you
as Mother Teresa loved you.

Here in the dark,
if only for these few silent night hours
let me walk with her
in your footsteps.

Let me know
what it is like
to love you unconditionally.

Let me love you
as she loved you.
As you love me.

Day Fifteen

My Day Begins

"Jesus' love for us is
unconditional,
tender,
forgiving,
complete."

Jesus' love for us is tender.

Tender is not a theologian's word.
It is not the word of a scholar

seeking to define the love of God.
It is the word of someone
caught up in the pain of humanity,
the word of a woman who has seen
God reach out to
heal that pain,
and joined him in the healing.

It is the daring word of an extraordinary woman
who knows from experience
that her God is not an uncaring distant God.

Mother Teresa saw God
and her God is a tender God.

A gentle God.

A caring God.

A God who knows our pain
and does not turn his face away.
A God who loves us
with a tender love.

Above all
a God who asks us
to love those in pain
with a tender love.

To love them
as he loves them,
as he loves us.

All Through the Day

He loves us with a tender love.

My Day Is Ending

Here in the dark silence of this night,
remind me
as I surrender to the quiet
that I am loved with a tender love
that only you can give.

But remind me too
that it is not enough to be loved.
I must love in return.
And love in kind.

Tenderness received
must become tenderness given.

Even as you share
in the pain of our common humanity,
so must I.
Tenderly.

Even as you reach out
to heal our common pain,
so must I.
Tenderly.

In the streets of the city,
Mother Teresa saw you,
saw and shared your tenderness.
So must I.

Day Sixteen

My Day Begins

"Jesus' love for us is
unconditional,
tender,
forgiving,
complete."

Jesus' love for us is a forgiving love.

We do not travel alone.
God travels with us.

At the start of our spiritual journey
and at every step along its way
our inseparable companion is
God's forgiving love.

With it he meets our need to love
and gives us his assurance that we are loved.

With it he meets our need to forgive
and gives us his assurance that we are forgiven.

We learn from him that
love and forgiveness are inseparable.
To love is to forgive.
To forgive is to love.
We cannot love without forgiving
or forgive with a loveless heart.

At the same time
the way God loves us becomes
a model for the way in which
we are to love each other.

We are to love as we have been loved.

We are to forgive as we have been forgiven.

All Through the Day

We forgive as we have been forgiven.

My Day Is Ending

Since I was a small child
with nothing but memorized words
to grow on,
I have been asking you to forgive
my trespasses
as I forgive those
who trespass against me.

Such big words for a child.
Words that need to be grown into.
And I wonder here in the night:
"Am I there yet?"

And I know the answer.
Tucked away in corners of my soul,

safely out of sight,
is a whole world of trespasses forgotten,
but not yet forgiven.

Here in the night
refresh my memory.

My father,
who art in heaven,
you have forgiven me every day of my life.
Now it's my turn
to forgive as I have been forgiven.

May your kingdom come,
your will be done,
On earth as it is in heaven.

Day Seventeen

My Day Begins

"Jesus' love for us is
unconditional,
tender,
forgiving,
complete."

■

Jesus' love for us is complete.

In a lifetime that leaves us so often
with an aching emptiness,

with a sense that there is something missing
at the heart of our being
we discover
with the help of Mother Teresa
what that "something" is.

We discover that
what we have been missing for a lifetime is
a sense of God present
at the center of our lives.
A sense of God completing us,
A sense of God fulfilling our humanity.

We discover that God's love for us is complete.

It is an extraordinary discovery.

For the first time
we feel whole.
For the first time
we feel a sense of completeness
that only God can give.
that only God can sustain.

It is not just that God loves us completely,
it is that he is our completion.

God loves us completely.
He always has.

All Through the Day

God's love for us is complete.

My Day Is Ending

Here in the deepening silence of this night
I know that your love for me is complete,
you hold nothing back.

But I don't act that way, do I?

I am still afraid of the dark,
still afraid
to surrender all of me.

There are still whole corners of my life
where I do not expect to find you.

There are still whole parts of me
that I do not expect you to love.

But your love is complete.
Mine is cautious and guarded.

It is my love not yours
that must be marked incomplete.
Day in and day out,
even as I enter into this night,
I sell your love short.
And in my caution
I hold back my love
from those who stand most in need.

I remain careful of my love,
miserly with my service.

Day Eighteen

My Day Begins

"We must first live the life,
only then can we preach the life."

In any primer of the spiritual life
this simple admonition would have to be
on the first page.

It seems, and it is, simple enough:
Don't preach a spiritual life

until and unless
you are willing to live it.

But for all its simplicity
it is easy to miss the fullness
of the point that it makes,
the point that so many of us miss.

It is not enough
to talk a good life.
Talking a spiritual life
is not the same as living one.

Knowing the right words
is not enough.
It is not enough
to praise Mother Teresa and her sisters,

not enough to admire and praise
these servants of the homeless,
to praise their service.

Only service itself is enough.

In Mother Teresa's own words:
"We must first live the life,
only then can we preach the life. "

◆◆◆◆◆

All Through the Day

It is not enough to talk a good life.

◆◆◆◆◆

LOVE WITHOUT MEASURE

My Day Is Ending

Here in the deepening silence of this night
I can call myself
your loving servant.

But I cannot fool myself.

Where were you,
I will hear you say,
When I was alone,

when I was hungry and naked,

Where were you,
I will hear you ask,

When I was homeless?

And if I am honest
I will have to say:
I was at home.
My eyes were closed
to the pain of the streets,
to your pain,

to the pain of the least of your brothers and sisters.

I was asleep.
In the silent darkness of this night
open my eyes and ears
to the needs of those
I am tempted to forget.
Wake me.

LOVE WITHOUT MEASURE

Day Nineteen

My Day Begins

"We are supposed to preach
without preaching,
not by words,
but by our example,
by our actions."

■

Here is an irony.
On a day of pomp and circumstance,
the world honored Teresa of Calcutta

with its most worldly honors,
but even as it distributed its honors
the same world
would be forced to acknowledge
the irony of the occasion.

A prince would say:
"No ceremonies, no protestations, no displays,
no routines of prayer,
and no theorizing
can compare with the smallest act
of genuine and practical compassion
as a true reflection of personal faith."

The prince got it right.
The woman being honored by the world
was never more or less than

a woman of faith.
She was not from a world of
ceremonies, protestations, and displays,
but a simple woman
driven by a practical compassion
for the poor of the world.

She was from the street,
and she brought with her
the people of the street,
and their pain.

She also brought, as we must,
a heart of faith
centered in service.

All Through the Day

Compassion is driven by faith.

My Day Is Ending

Here in the deepening silence of this night
I am not so foolish as to believe
that a splash of
ceremonies, protestations, and displays,
awaits my act of faith,
my timid gestures of compassion.

More likely there would be surprise,
not just in others,
but in my own closed-in heart—
surprise that at long last
I had found room
for Mother Teresa's people.

But it is night
and dreams come easily.

A few hours from now
I will awake
with a willing but cautious heart
in a world too real
for my soul,
in a world of real streets, real pain,
real hunger.

Be with me then,
As I beg you to be with me now.

I need not be alone.
I am not dreaming
You are here.

It is your strength, not mine.

Day Twenty

■

My Day Begins

"In the end it is God's work
and you are just a weak instrument in his hands."

■

It is tempting to think
that the outcome of the spiritual journey
is in our hands—
something we do,
something we achieve,.
something our effort determines.

Mother Teresa knew better.

She described herself as
"just a little pencil in his hand
to be replaced when God found someone weaker."

Weaker, she said.
Not stronger.
Because strength is not at stake.
Faith is.
"In the end," she said, "It's God's work.
In the end we are just a weak instrument
in his hands."

The image of us as pencil in his hands
may seem like catechism theology,
a mere display of spiritual modesty,

but it is in fact
an image that goes to the very heart
of the spiritual journey.

Unlike any other part of our life
we measure spiritual success
not by what we achieve,
but by embracing
a process of
getting weaker by the day.

In the end
it is God,
not us,
who does what must be done.

All Through the Day

Only God can do what must be done.

My Day Is Ending

Here in the deepening silence of this night
I try to remember
what I did today
and what I didn't do.
I'm not sure why.

I know that in the end
it isn't even my work.
It is God's work,
your work,
and I am just a weak instrument
in your hands.

But I want it to matter.
I want to fall asleep

knowing that my day
has been worth something.
I want to wake to a day
that will make some difference
to somebody, somehow.

But that day will never come
as long as I
try to do it without you.

Day Twenty-One

My Day Begins

"To keep a lamp burning
we have to keep putting oil in it."

■

Tested by the unforgiving streets,
by broken hearts
and broken bodies,
by a world that never seems to change,
it is easy to let the fire go out,
easy to let our hearts go dry,
easy to turn away.

We are not strangers here.

We have watched, you and I,
in late night hours
As a candle of faith flickered and threatened to die.

We have watched a fire turn to ashes.
We have felt a chill
where just a moment ago there was warmth.

We have left the fire unstoked,
the candle unreplaced.
We have settled deeper into our security,
as the night overtook the flame.

We know that
no fire burns forever.
No fire burns unfueled.

Flames die.
So do souls.

A fire needs refueling.
"To keep a lamp burning
we have to keep putting oil in it."

It is time
to rekindle the flame.

All Through the Day

Faith needs refueling.

My Day Is Ending

Here in the deepening silence of this night
my faith, for a moment,
cuts through the darkness,
and the night chill.
I feel the warmth of your presence.

You promised to be here with me.
You are.
But in a moment,
unnoticed, untended,
the fire that warms this night
could become
ashes in the night.

The fire must be tended.

I must do my best to keep the fire alive,
the lamp burning.
I will.

But in the end I will have to depend on you.

You are the fire.
It is you who lights up the night.
It is you who gives us hope
in the darkness.

Here in the night
feed the fitful fire of my faith
with your presence,
with your promises.

It is you, only you,
who keeps the fire burning.

Day Twenty-Two

■

My Day Begins

"It is not how much we give
but how much we put into our giving."

■

As in so many other things,
it is not spiritual brilliance,
or some profound formula
that shapes our life.

It can be and often is
some basic imperishable cliche.

So when we hear Mother Teresa talk to her sisters
it is easy to miss in her commonplace words
the power
of what she has to say.

"It is not how much we give,"
she reminds them and us,
"but how much we put into our giving."

It doesn't get that much plainer than that.

It's not quantity.
It's heart.

Knowing this truth to be simple
doesn't make it any easier
to learn and live.

We need to embrace the obvious.

To get to the heart of the matter
we must first
abandon our need, our taste for the novel,
and the scintillating.

Simple as it may seem,
we either put our whole self into our giving,
or it is not worth it.

All Through the Day

We can't play it safe.

My Day Is Ending

Here in the deepening silence of this night
a part of me still expects
some brilliant burst of light,
some dramatic demand for more.

But like the day,
the night never catches fire.
There should be more.
Nothing I do ever seems
to be enough.

A part of me wants to know
what more you expect of me.

I am not asking for more,
I hear you say.

It is not how much you give,
I hear you say,
but how much you put into your giving.
It is not how much you give
of what you have
that matters,
it is how much of who you are.

So I accept who I am
and what I have.

In the long run
it is all I have to give.

Day Twenty-Three

■

My Day Begins

"I see God in every human being.
When I wash the leper's wounds,
I feel I am nursing the Lord himself.
Is it not a beautiful experience?"

■

As much as I want to say, "Yes, yes, it is beautiful,"
I know that for me and for many, if not most of us,
the service of the poor and dying
is not a beautiful experience.
It demands that we cut through

layers of repugnance and fear,
that we face up to a world from which
we would prefer to turn our eyes away.

When we look for God in the face of a leper
there is I think a secret hope that the wounds will go away,
by some miracle of divine alchemy
it will become what it will never be.
But the spirituality of Mother Teresa
is not a spirituality of miracles.
What we find almost impossible to look at
will not go away,
will not be sweetened, dressed up for the occasion,
will not become a thing of beauty.
In Mother Teresa's world it doesn't happen that way.
It is the raw, disturbing, wounded body of a human being

that we are expected to love.
We are not supposed to lie to ourselves
that this is something pretty,
but rather to love humanity as it is,
frail, wounded, unpleasant to see or to touch.
We should not expect that by our mere desire,
by our prayers, reality will become what it is not.

Our prayers come down to this:
I didn't recognize you at first.
You are not what I expected.
But now I hope that I would recognize you anywhere, in anyone.

All Through the Day

I would recognize you anywhere.

My Day Is Ending

Here in the growing darkness
remind me that the night, this night,
is not meant to be a hiding place,
not a place to wrap hard truths in soft words.

I must love you as I find you.
I must love you in the wounded histories,
in the broken bodies and souls
of real human beings, in the humanity that is.
But not only in pain, in happiness too—
in the love stories of our lives, in dreams fulfilled,
in hopes blossoming with every new day,
in the lives of those we love,
in the unexpected greeting of a passing stranger.

In a child born to be loved.
You are everywhere your children are.
I may not recognize you at first.
You may not be whom I expected.
But here in the darkness I pray that I will recognize you,
that I will not pass you by.

Day Twenty-Four

My Day Begins

"If you are really in love with Christ
no matter how small your work,
it will be done better.
It will be wholehearted."

We need to be honest with ourselves.
We need to keep our expectations in their proper place.
We are not going to be another Mother Teresa.
The Nobel Prize is not in our future.

World leaders and movie stars
are unlikely to notice us.

Even at the end of this work-filled day
and a thousand others like it
we will not be recognized
and thanked.

It's hard to accept.

The part of us that needs
to hear a word of praise, of thanks, of congratulations
will have to do without.
It's not going to happen.
Some days will have their own satisfactions,
but chances are
they will seem not enough
to give meaning to every day.

It will be tempting to look for something
with more payback.
It will be tempting
to live, to serve
halfheartedly.

But, "If you are really in love with Christ," she said,
"no matter how small your work,
it will be done better.
It will be wholehearted."

That's what it is all about, isn't it?
Learning to serve
with a whole heart.

◆◆◆◆◆

All Through the Day

To live with a whole heart is to serve.

◆◆◆◆◆

My Day Is Ending

Here in the deepening silence of this night
I need not be reminded
that no one is waiting here to say:
Thank you. Congratulations. Nice going.

This day will pass unpraised.
Night will fall silently.
Whatever small service I have given this day
will go unmarked,
unnoticed, it may seem, even by you.

But if I have really put my heart
at your service,
my whole heart,
however unnoticed my day,

it will have been done better
for having been done for you.

It doesn't matter whether anyone noticed.

That's what I need to remember
in the quiet of this night.
I need to be honest with you,
with myself.

You are not asking me to be Mother Teresa,
just me.
Wholeheartedly.

Day Twenty-Five

■

My Day Begins

"If we have no peace,
it is because we have forgotten
that we belong to each other."

■

When the world came to honor her,
it was with a peace prize.
What did she know about peace
that we, all of us,
so desperately need to learn?

We need to learn,
in Mother Teresa's strangely powerful language,
a simple truth that underlay her wisdom and her life.

We belong to each other.

We pay,
the world pays,
a terrible price
when we forget what she taught.

There is no peace,
there can be no peace,
neither in our hearts
nor in the world,
until we accept
that we belong to each other.

Peace disappears, becomes impossible,
at that moment when we try
to separate ourselves from one another,
when we try to go it alone,
when we make it a synonym for quiet and solitude,
for a protected heart,
a safe life.

We belong to that hungry woman,
that homeless child,
to all those in need.
And they belong to us.

Peace is our prize.

All Through the Day

We belong to each other.

My Day Is Ending

Here in the deepening silence of this night
I wonder whether I will ever find the peace
for which I so deeply yearn.

This quiet silence
is not enough.

My heart wants more.

But the truth is that
I am not ready for a peace
such as Mother Teresa knew.

I have not forgotten
that we belong to each other,
but I am not ready to pay
the price for peace.

I am not ready
to belong to the world,
not ready
to let the world into my heart.

But until I belong to you,
until I accept that you belong to me,

there will be no peace.
There is no easy way.
There is no way that does not
embrace the world.

Day Twenty-Six

My Day Begins

"Never, ever, get discouraged."

We read her words
and we find ourselves saying,
Easy for you to say!

On any given morning
when it seems that the best we can hope for
is just another unpromising day,

being told not to get discouraged
can sound like so much pious chatter,
a vacuous substitute
for the reality out of which
we must carve some kind of spirituality.

Our task is to get up on that morning—
on this morning—on any morning—
when everything in our soul tells us to stay in bed,
when everything in our soul
tells us that we cannot even think
about the street and its poverty.

It's time to remember something
that Mother Teresa never forgot.

Let's not flatter ourselves.

Some things will always be beyond us.
Whatever gets done will be done
by the God who is forever at work
in our lives,
and in the hearts of the street-bound poor.

We need to get up
and admit that it's not our day.
It doesn't have to be.
It's God's day.
It always is.

A character in one of Samuel Beckett's plays says:
"You must go on,
I can't go on,
I'll go on."

All Through the Day

Never, ever, get discouraged.

My Day Is Ending

Here in the growing darkness of this night
I remind myself
that it takes courage to get through the day,
more courage than I have most days.

But when I prayed for courage today
all I could hear was Mother Teresa saying:
"Never, ever, get discouraged."
But I do.
My courage is at best a sometimes thing.

I can feel it here
in the unchallenged silence of the night.
But I know that it will evaporate with the dawn
and the sharp-edged realities
of the day to come,
the day that is just hours away.

I think about tomorrow.
I wonder: "What did she know
that I have never learned?
What is the secret of her courage?

I think it is because
she never entered a day alone.
She never felt that it was all up to her.

She never forgot
that God was with her all the way.
I forget,
yet God waits for me to pray.

He waits for me to grow
prayer by prayer, into his likeness—
the very likeness of God.

Day Twenty-Seven

My Day Begins

"The beginning of prayer is silence . . .
God speaks in the silence of our heart.
and to the silence of our heart.
And he listens."

■

It is difficult for us to understand that
for Mother Teresa, for anyone,
serving the needy begins
not in activity, but in prayer.

Before we can serve
we have to learn how to be silent,
how to listen,
how to do nothing,
how to pray.

Only in silence,
only in prayer,
can we hear the voices seeking
to be heard above the noise of our lives.
Only in silence can we hear the voice of God
above our own ambitions, above our pride.
Only in silence can we hear the voice of our own spiritual
hunger,
and the voices of those who live in need.

It is not easy for us.
There is so much to be done.
So little time. So many in need.

We have been taught that if we don't do it, nobody will.
Mother Teresa, however, knows better.
Before we can do anything for anyone
we need to silence our hearts.

Without that silence,
without prayer,
without listening,
our service will be crippled
before we even begin.

All Through the Day

In the beginning there is silence.

My Day Is Ending

Another silent night has come.

It is time to put the day to rest,
time to let this night's darkness
surround me
with its silence.

It is time to let God speak,
time for me to listen for him,
in the hunger of my soul,
in the voices of the voiceless
in the patient silence of the night.

It is time to let go of the day,
time to silence my heart.

It is time to pray.

Not with words
But in silence.
With silence.
Let us pray.

Day Twenty-Eight

My Day Begins

"To pray is
to allow God to come alive in us."

A life of service begins with prayer.

It begins at that moment
when we understand that in some profoundly mysterious way
God is reachable,
not just with the rote words and gestures of our childhood,
but with the spontaneous movements

of our changing and hungry heart,
with its expansions and contractions,
with our acknowledgement that God is within us,
waiting to be touched by our hopes and fears.

God waits—
in the poignant and powerful insight of Mother Teresa—
to be brought alive.
God waits to come alive within us.
He waits for us to pray.
He waits for us
to grow prayer by prayer into his likeness,
into the likeness of God.

This is what prayer is about.
Prayer is the nourishment of our spirit,
even as our growth becomes the measure of our prayer.

LOVE WITHOUT MEASURE

The more we pray,
that is, the more we allow God to live within us,
the more we grow in his likeness.

It is Mother Teresa who has taught us this relationship.
More to the point,
it is Mother Teresa who has lived it,
who has demonstrated its truth.
She has allowed God
to come alive within her.
On the poverty ridden streets of the world's great cities
she steadily grew before our eyes
in the image and likeness of God.

It is she who now coaxes us to pray.

All Through the Day

Come alive in us.

My Day Is Ending

Here in the dark silence of this night
I wait for my prayers
to bring you alive within me.

Teach me how to pray.

Help me to get beyond
the tidy words of my childhood.

Help me to reach that place
where you live within me,
where you wait for me,
where my hopes and fears reach out to touch you.

You wait for me to grow
prayer by prayer,
into your likeness.

Teach my changing and hungry heart,
with all its expansions and contractions,
how to pray.

The more
I allow you
to live in me,
the more I grow in your likeness.

Come alive in me.

Day Twenty-Nine

■

My Day Begins

"My secret is a very simple one. I pray."

■

Mother Teresa tells an interviewer
that her spiritual secret is no great secret: she prays.

And she will pardon us, we hope,
if the first image we conjure up
is a classically frail, white-habited nun
on her knees,
in some place of silence and solitude,

begging for favors
from a generous father.

That's what we would do.

But then she tells us
what prayer is.

"Prayer is not asking.
Prayer is putting one's self in the hands of God.
Prayer is surrendering,
is letting go."

Prayer is that same
frail, white habited woman
not with her hands folded in piety,
but open in surrender,

not closeted
but outstretched in service.

Prayer is putting one's self
in the hands of God.
Because the sum of human pain
is too much
for any human heart.

Accept what I have to give, she prays,
and do with it what only you can do.

All Through the Day

Prayer is surrender.

My Day Is Ending

Here in the growing darkness
I find myself reaching out for words
with which to pray,
with which to catch the ear of God,
your ear.

I know better.
I know that it is not about words.
It is all about
putting myself in your hands.

But I am not there yet.
I need familiar words to reassure me.

I need to know that you hear
what is in my heart.

I need to remember
that all I have to do is surrender
and put my life in your hands.

You do not need my words,
but I still do.

I am using words.
I know it.
Hear me.

Day Thirty

My Day Begins

"We all need to be converted . . .
to accept God in our lives.
But unless we change our hearts
there is no conversion.
Changing places is not the answer,
changing occupations is not the answer.
The answer is to change our hearts."

■

The chances that you or I will spend our days
on Calcutta's streets or America's equivalent

are very slim indeed.
We know this—you and I.
But we also know that in some profound and pressing way
Mother Teresa has not left us off the hook.

Her message is not about moving to Calcutta.
Nor about becoming a nun.

It is about a radical change of heart,
a radical recentering of our soul.
It is about conversion.

And specifically it is about
a conversion to a spirituality of service
that will demand not just a change in our lives,
but a change that affects other lives.

For Mother Teresa conversion means
inviting God into our hearts and lives
along with all those who accompany him
wherever he goes.

In the world where Mother Teresa lives
God never comes alone.
He always arrives accompanied by his friends:
the hungry, the naked,
the homeless,
and the helpless.

All Through the Day

God always brings his friends.

My Day Is Ending

Here as the night begins
and I seek the silence and peace of sleep,
there are voices that cannot,
must not, be stilled.

They are the voices of the hungry,
the naked, the homeless,
and the helpless.

They are the voices of the poor,
the powerless.
They are your voice.
You must be heard
because they must be heard.

So let me listen here in this night
to hear,
beyond the silence
and the stillness
the voices that must be heard.

Let me hear them.
Let me hear you.

Remind me that
love cannot remain silent.

The silence must be broken.

The voices must be heard.

One Final Word

This book has been written not as a final word but as a gateway to the spiritual wisdom of a specific teacher, a gateway opening up our own spiritual path.

Some, inspired by her example, may choose a life of service, following her step by step into the streets of the world's great and troubled cities. For most of us, however, it will be enough to discover and live the truth that love and service cannot be separated. That there is love, peace, and joy even in the world's most troubled streets.

To all of us she will have said something that is critical to our spiritual growth.

You may decide that Mother Teresa is someone whose experience of God is one that you wish to follow more closely and deeply.

You may, on the other hand, decide that her experience and wisdom has not helped you. There are many other teachers.

Somewhere there is the right teacher for your own, very special, absolutely unique journey of the spirit. You *will* find your teacher; you *will* discover your path. We would not be searching, as St. Augustine reminds us, if we had not already been found.

One more thing should be said.

Spirituality is not meant to be self-absorption, a cocoon-like relationship between God and me. In the long run, if it is to have meaning, if it is to grow and deepen and not wither, it must be a wellspring of compassionate living. It must reach out to others as God has reached out to us.

True spirituality breaks down the walls of our soul to let in not just heaven, but the whole world.

You May Want to Read

Words To Love By . . . Mother Teresa. (Ave Maria Press. Notre Dame, IN). She once complained about words. "Too many words," she said. "Let them just see what we do." Yet she continued to speak, patiently repeating the essentials of her vision. You will find many of her words in these pages.